PEOPLE POWER
CAMPAIGNS & CAUSES

David Downing

H www.heinemann.co.uk/library
Visit our website to find out more information about Heinemann Library books.

To order:
☎ Phone 44 (0) 1865 888066
🖹 Send a fax to 44 (0) 1865 314091
💻 Visit the Heinemann Bookshop at www.heinemann.co.uk/library to browse our catalogue and order online.

First published in Great Britain by Heinemann Library,
Halley Court, Jordan Hill, Oxford OX2 8EJ,
a division of Reed Educational and Professional Publishing Ltd.
Heinemann is a registered trademark of Reed Educational and Professional Publishing Ltd.

OXFORD MELBOURNE AUCKLAND
JOHANNESBURG BLANTYRE GABORONE
IBADAN PORTSMOUTH (NH) USA CHICAGO

Designed by AMR
Originated by Dot Gradations
Printed in Hong Kong by South China Printing

ISBN 0 431 12435 3 (hardback)
06 05 04 03 02
10 9 8 7 6 5 4 3 2 1

British Library Cataloguing in Publication Data

Downing, David
  People power : campaigns and causes. – (Political & economic systems)
  1. Social movements – Juvenile literature 2. Political participation – Juvenile literature
  I. Title
  322.4

Acknowledgements
The publishers would like to thank the following for permission to reproduce photographs:
Corbis: pp. 10, 14, 17, 27, 44, 50, 54; Hulton Archive: pp. 5, 9, 13, 16, 18, 20, 21, 24, 26, 29, 30, 34, 37, 40; PA Photos: pp. 6, 38; Popperfoto: pp. 46, 52; Rex: pp. 33, 39, 43, 47, 49.

Cover photograph: Suffragettes marching for women's right to vote, reproduced with permission of Corbis.

Every effort has been made to contact copyright holders of any material reproduced in this book. Any omissions will be rectified in subsequent printings if notice is given to the publishers.

Our thanks to Christopher Gibb for his comments in the preparation of this book.

Contents

1   Filling the square   4

2   Where do campaigns and causes come from?   6

3   How campaigns are fought   12

4   Slavery and race equality   18

5   Women and children last   23

6   Helping the less fortunate   28

7   The treatment of animals   32

8   Conflicting interests   36

9   Matters of life and death   40

10   Single-issue political parties   45

11   International campaigns   48

12   So, what are causes and campaigns?   53

Timeline   56

Further reading, sources and websites   59

Glossary   61

Index   64

Any words appearing in the text in bold, **like this**, are explained in the glossary.

① Filling the square

October 1908. Thousands of people, most of them women, have crowded into London's Trafalgar Square to attend a rally of the Women's Social and Political Union, the main **suffragette** group campaigning for women's right to vote.

This is obviously a political event – the speakers on the platform are demanding political changes – but it has nothing to do with political parties. On other days the women crammed into the square might support particular policies of the main parties of the time, but today they are simply women who want the vote. This desire also overrides differences of age, region and class – young factory girls from the north stand side by side with elderly duchesses from the Home Counties.

The leaders speak, the audience cheers. Off to the side, stalls are selling badges, rosettes and pamphlets putting forward the women's arguments. Their campaign has been going on for decades, and still has twenty years to run before British women finally achieve voting equality with men.

Fifty years later, the same square. The recently formed **Campaign for Nuclear Disarmament** (CND) is holding a rally, and this time men and women are both present in large numbers. Again, people of all political persuasions, ages and classes listen to speeches and pore over the stalls selling campaign literature and badges. This group of people is also united by a single overpowering belief, that nuclear weapons are both morally indefensible and profoundly dangerous. In 1958, it is hoping to persuade the British people and the British government to share this belief. CND will still be hoping and campaigning at the start of the 21st century.

Over the years, many other campaigning groups have used Trafalgar Square – and other such squares around the world – to get their messages out through the megaphones and microphones: save the children, save the tiger, save the planet.

Where do these groups come from and how do they operate? Why do there seem to be so many more of them with each passing year, and why can't ordinary party politics deal with the issues they raise? Where do campaigns and causes come from?

CND supporters gather in London's Trafalgar Square after their annual Easter march from Aldermaston to London, 30 March 1959.

Where do campaigns and causes come from?

A cause is a political aim or objective which an individual or group wants to achieve, and a campaign is the continuous, organized effort which that individual or group makes to reach it. For example, one cause which many British people have pursued is an end to fox-hunting, and their campaign has included holding many meetings, writing countless letters and mounting numerous protests.

Most of the campaigns explored in this book, like the one to ban fox-hunting, are single-issue campaigns – that is, they are mainly concerned with changing how society works in one particular way. They are not interested in the wider issues concerning how society organizes itself socially or economically. In order to persuade other people that the changes they want will benefit society as a whole, the campaigners usually organize themselves in pressure groups. They are called pressure groups because their aim is to pressurize governments or other powerful organizations into introducing the changes they want.

Boxing Day 1997: anti-blood-sport campaigners jeer at a passing huntsman in Maldon, Essex.

Campaigning pressure groups v. political parties

Campaigning pressure groups differ from political parties in two obvious ways. Firstly, they usually concentrate on one issue, whereas political parties have to deal with all the issues which the **electorate** are interested in, and many which they are not. Secondly, pressure groups want to influence government, whereas political parties want to become the government.

Temperance

The temperance, or anti-alcohol, campaigns which took place in many countries in the late 19th and early 20th centuries were classic single-issue campaigns. The introduction of **Prohibition** in 1920 marked the success of the campaign in the USA, but the law proved impossible to enforce, and in 1933 the drinking of alcohol was made legal once more.

Campaigning pressure groups also differ from what are usually called interest groups – organizations like **trade unions** and **professional bodies**. Only miners can join the National Union of Mineworkers, only doctors can belong to the British Medical Association, and the main reason for the existence of such organizations is to further the interests of their own members. Campaigning pressure groups are open to everyone, and although they sometimes exist to pursue the interest of a particular section of society, their members usually believe – in many cases, rightly – that they are also serving the overall interests of society as a whole.

Getting together

What gets a campaign started? Firstly, a significant number of people must come, for one reason or another, to share the feeling that something badly needs changing. Secondly, those people must believe that their government has no intention of introducing the changes they desire – if it had, there would be no need for a campaign. For example, the **suffragette** movement, which campaigned

7

for women's right to vote in the early years of the 20th century, knew that the major political parties of the time were opposed to the female vote. Therefore they had no choice but to launch their own campaigning group outside **Parliament**.

In some cases, one party does agree with the aims of a campaigning group. The British Labour Party, for example, came out in favour of a ban on fox-hunting in its election manifestos in both 1997 and 2001. So why did those who opposed fox-hunting not abandon their own groups and join the Labour Party? There were several reasons. One, a person opposed to fox-hunting might have disagreed with the Labour Party's policy on other issues. Two, the Labour Party might change its mind on fox-hunting, or give the issue a lower priority than the campaigner wanted. Three, the Labour Party might lose an election, and be replaced by a party which had no intention of banning fox-hunting. For all these reasons, it was far better to keep anti-hunting pressure groups in existence. These groups could keep up the pressure on government from outside, and no matter what any particular government chose to do, they could be sure of keeping the issue in the public eye.

Campaigning for what?

Pressure groups flourish when governments have to listen to the people, and the slow spread of **democracy** over the last two centuries has seen a huge rise in their number, importance and variety. Campaigns have been fought over a bewildering range of issues, from world peace to the building of a by-pass around a town, from the abolition of **slavery** to an ending of the trade in animal furs. These campaigns can be categorized, or divided up, in a number of ways.

One way is by their geographical spread. Some campaigns have been conducted around the world, some within the borders of a particular nation, while others have been fought out in a single village.

Chartism

The British Chartists were unusual in being multi-issue campaigners. Their six goals, as spelt out in the People's Charter of 1838, were votes for all men (at the time only a small percentage of men could vote), elections every year, secret ballots, equal-sized electoral districts, payment for MPs, and the removal of the need for MPs to own a certain amount of property. Their campaign, which lasted ten years and contained several violent episodes, failed to achieve any of these ends (although all but yearly elections were achieved in later years). One reason given for the Chartists' failure was their lack of focus on a single issue.

Chartist speakers address a crowd on London's Kennington Common in 1848.

Another way is by historical order, but there is a difficulty here. Few campaigns have had neat beginnings and ends. Many have grown out of old campaigns and then created the conditions for new ones. The anti-slavery campaign of the mid-19th century, for example, eventually led to the **civil rights** campaign of the mid-20th century. In one sense, they were both episodes in a longer campaign for racial equality.

Campaigns can also be categorized according to whether or not they are ever likely to end. A campaign to prevent the building of a new by-pass usually comes to an end when a final decision is made to abandon or go ahead with the project, whereas the campaign to end cruelty to animals seems likely to last for ever. This is partly because definitions of cruelty change with time. Forms of treatment considered acceptable by most people at the beginning of the 19th century had become unacceptable to most people 200 years later.

An anti-hunting demonstration in Virginia, USA. Protestors hold up signs condemning deer-hunting with bows and arrows.

Campaigns can be divided according to how seriously their success would affect the society. Giving women the vote may have annoyed many men at the time, but it did not fundamentally alter the way political democracy worked. Accepting that animals have equal rights to humans, would, on the other hand, involve huge changes in the way humans live their lives.

Finally, the campaigns of the last two centuries can be arranged – as they are in this book – by subject, by what they are actually about. Many are concerned with the way people treat each other, whether on racial grounds (chapter 4), gender or age grounds (chapter 5) or on grounds of economic and social success (chapter 6). There are issues which arise from the way humans treat other species (chapter 7) and those which involve two sections of society with conflicting interests (chapter 8). A specific example of the latter are those **moral issues** which involve the taking of life (chapter 9). Finally, there are political parties which have come together around particular issues (chapter 10) and those new international causes and campaigns which have sprung up in the wake of **globalization** (chapter 11).

Firstly, though, we must take a more general look at how campaigns have come together, and how they have been conducted.

3 How campaigns are fought

In the late 20th and early 21st centuries, causes and campaigns tend to be connected in the public mind with organized groups like Greenpeace, Amnesty International or, in the USA, the National Rifle Association. Sometimes these organizations, which are often known as non-governmental organizations, or NGOs, have spokespeople whom we recognize, but generally, today's causes are not represented by individuals.

Lone campaigners

This was not the case in the early 19th century, when individuals were more likely to play a crucial role in bringing a particular cause to the attention of the public and the government. The English prison reformer Elizabeth Fry was a good example of how one person's activities could grow into a campaign involving many people. Her **Quaker** family was rich, but a visit by a Quaker from the USA inspired her to seek out and help the poor children of a nearby village. Having married and moved to London, she heard about the terrible conditions in nearby Newgate Prison and decided to improve them. She collected clothing for the babies who lived with their imprisoned mothers, and started a school for both mothers and children. Slowly but surely, Newgate Prison became a place where prisoners were allowed to prepare themselves for a useful life in the world outside.

The power of the pen

In the mid-19th century, novels played the same sort of role that radio, TV and film do today in raising public awareness of particular issues. Charles Dickens was particularly good at dramatizing issues like the treatment of abused children and the poor in his stories. For example, his description in *Nicholas Nickleby* of a private school in which abandoned children were badly mistreated caused a public outcry, and led to a campaign for the abolition of such terrible schools.

There were many other famous campaigning individuals during this period. Lord Shaftesbury, for example, worked for several decades to improve working conditions in the new factories created by the Industrial Revolution in Britain. The Englishman William Tuke and the Frenchman Philippe Pinel campaigned for more understanding treatment of the mentally ill, and Americans like Frederick Douglass, John Brown and Harriet Beecher Stowe all campaigned, in very different ways, against slavery in their country.

Groups, members and funds

The principal opponents of the **slave trade** and **slavery**, however, were organized groups like the British Society for Abolition of the Slave Trade (founded 1787) and the American Anti-Slavery Society (1832). Groups like these, and the many thousands of others which have appeared since then, are brought into existence by like-minded people who feel strongly about their particular causes – so strongly, in fact, that they are ready to give up their time (in meetings and demonstrations) and their money (in donations and membership fees) to fight for the changes they desire.

On the way to his own execution, US anti-slavery campaigner John Brown takes time to kiss an African American baby.

Once such a group has been formed, and the various offices – a chairperson to run meetings, a secretary to keep records, a treasurer to look after the money, a public relations person to deal with the media – have been filled, the first priority is often growth. The bigger the group, the more influence it will have on both government and public. The bigger the group, the wider the range of skills and expertise which it will probably contain. The bigger the group, the more income it will receive in membership fees.

Campaigning groups cannot survive without funds. Publicity – producing leaflets, hiring halls for meetings, placing ads in papers and on TV – costs money. Research – which is often needed to provide telling facts and convincing evidence – costs money. Going to court, either as a **plaintiff** or a defendant, often costs money. The famous American civil rights campaigner Martin Luther King Jr spent a large proportion of his time raising funds to pay the **civil rights** campaign's legal costs.

It is true that some long-term campaigns for helping the less fortunate – Age Concern and Oxfam, for example – are given some financial support by governments, but most campaigning groups are engaged in a constant struggle to cover their own expenses.

Raising money is always a critical issue for campaigning groups. Here, two Salvation Army trumpeters play for donations in front of Macy's, a New York department store.

Influencing the politicians

Once organized and funded, the groups have to get their message across to the people that matter. In democracies, the government is obviously the main target. It can be approached in a number of ways – directly, indirectly through **Parliament**, or more indirectly still through the public, who have the final say in which governments are elected.

For a group to influence government directly, it must be in communication with government ministers or those officials who work for them. A group like Shelter, which campaigns for the homeless, can expect to be consulted by government whenever a new measure is introduced in their field. This is partly because Shelter has a great deal of knowledge and expertise, and partly because the government wants to avoid criticism from such a respected group. Members of Shelter might be invited to join working groups preparing new measures and laws, or to help with the administration of those measures and laws once they have been introduced.

Few groups have this sort of direct influence. Most use Parliament to spread their message. They can of course put up candidates in parliamentary elections, but generally speaking, the public has preferred traditional party candidates to those representing a single issue. It is easier to write to MPs who are known to sympathize with the cause in question, and to ask them to raise the issue in Parliament whenever they can. The pressure groups can also employ full-time parliamentary **lobbyists** – people who are paid to persuade individual MPs to support a particular cause. And, as a last resort, there is always the mass lobby, in which the group brings its supporters – sometimes numbering in the thousands – to demonstrate in front of the Parliament building. This was a favourite tactic of the British **suffragettes**, and often led to pitched battles between police and demonstrators in London's Parliament Square.

Influencing the public

When it comes to influencing the public, there are many ways open to the campaigning groups. They can organize mass marches and demonstrations like the famous marches of the late 1950s, or the August 1963 march on Washington which ended with Martin Luther King Jr's famous 'I have a dream' speech. They can organize spectacular publicity stunts, or encourage popular celebrities to announce their support for the cause. They can advertise themselves directly, pay for research which further strengthens their argument, or start **legal test cases** against those they accuse of wrongdoing.

Civil rights leader Martin Luther King Jr waves to the Washington crowd after delivering his 'I have a dream' speech on 28 August 1963. Mass marches like this one bring a campaign to people's attention.

They can try to get their message across to the young by providing speakers for schools. They can take direct physical action against their opponents, like the Greenpeace supporters who have tried to interfere with the activities of those engaged in whaling and underwater nuclear tests, or the anti-by-pass protesters who have occupied trees and tunnels above and below the route of proposed new roads.

They can even resort to violence against people or property, as some animal rights groups, frustrated by their lack of progress, have done in recent years.

Demonstrators from Greenpeace use a raft full of oil-covered inflatable animals to point out the dangers of oil-drilling in the waters around Florida.

Whichever tactics a group chooses, it will choose them with the media in mind. Elizabeth Fry and Lord Shaftesbury no doubt studied the newspapers for signs that their campaigns were changing people's minds, and today's campaigners know that television reporting is crucial to their success. Events are frequently organized for the benefit of the cameras, and spokespeople are always on hand to repeat the campaigners' arguments and demands.

4 Slavery and racial equality

The first African slaves arrived in the Americas around 1517, only a quarter of a century after Columbus, but it was the later growth of **plantation** economies in the West Indies (mainly sugar) and the southern states (rice, tobacco and cotton) which created the booming slave trade of the 17th and 18th centuries. Many European ports grew rich on the trade, and plantation owners across the Atlantic enjoyed lives of luxury and ease through their brutal exploitation of another race.

Abolishing the slave trade

There were always a few individuals who spoke out against slavery, but it was not until the late 18th century that their numbers began to grow. Many of **slavery's** first opponents, in both Britain and the American **colonies**, were members of the **Quaker** religious group. It was Pennsylvania, originally established as a Quaker colony, which in 1780 became the first state of the newly independent USA to begin freeing its slaves.

In Britain, a small group of Christian **evangelists** in London led the fight against slavery and the slave trade. One of their number, Granville Sharp, led a one-man campaign against slavery in Britain itself, and in 1772 he managed to prove his point by getting a court to give a runaway slave his freedom. Fifteen years later, Sharp was elected chairman of the newly founded Society for the Abolition of the **Slave Trade**, but it was another member of the evangelist group, Thomas Clarkson, who really ran the Society.

Thomas Clarkson addresses a meeting of the Anti-Slavery Society at London's Freemason's Hall. His campaign against slavery was the first successful pressure group campaign of modern times.

Over the next twenty years Clarkson organized what one historian (F. E. Huggett in his *Slaves and Slavery*) called the first successful pressure group campaign of modern times.

First, Clarkson collected the facts about the slave trade, because he and his friends were convinced that if people really knew what was happening, they would oppose it. Many pamphlets and books were published, and **petitions** were presented to **Parliament**. People were encouraged to stop buying things produced by slave labour, like West Indian sugar and rum.

The campaign worked slowly, but it worked. With each passing year there were more people who disapproved of the slave trade. Another crucial member of the Society, the Yorkshire MP William Wilberforce, kept raising the issue in Parliament. In 1807 a law was finally passed abolishing the slave trade – the buying and selling of slaves – in all British possessions. Existing slaves were not set free, however, and in 1823 Clarkson and Wilberforce helped form a new campaigning pressure group, the Anti-Slavery Society. This time it only took them ten years. Slavery was abolished in all British possessions in 1833.

Abolishing slavery in the USA

The situation in the USA was more complicated, in that each state was allowed to choose whether or not it allowed slavery within its borders. The northern states, which were busy industrializing by the 1830s, had no need of slaves, but the huge cotton and tobacco **plantations** of the South would become unprofitable if the existing slaves were freed.

In 1832 the American Anti-Slavery Society was formed in Philadelphia, and over the next 30 years its campaigns helped to convince a majority of Americans that slavery was wrong. Several important individuals were also involved, and each helped the cause of anti-slavery in their own way.

Harriet Beecher Stowe's novel, *Uncle Tom's Cabin*, which was published in 1852, brought home to many people just how terrible slavery was. The escaped slave Frederick Douglass campaigned tirelessly between 1841 and the outbreak of the American Civil War twenty years later, and his autobiography *The Narrative of the Life of Frederick Douglass, An American Slave* became a best-seller. In 1859 John Brown and his supporters attacked and captured a government armoury at Harpers Ferry in Virginia in the vain hope that this would start a slave revolt. Brown was captured and hanged, but he had shown the USA that anti-slavery was a cause which some Americans were ready to die for.

Eva comforts the child slave Topsy in a scene from Harriet Beecher Stowe's powerful anti-slavery novel *Uncle Tom's Cabin*.

The continuing fight for racial equality

By 1861, a majority of Americans had become convinced that slavery was too important an issue for individual states to decide, and the civil war was fought to enforce this view. After the North's victory the slaves were set free.

In theory African Americans could now enjoy the same rights as other Americans, but in fact this was rarely the case. Particularly in the South, they were kept in a permanently inferior position.

Other campaigning groups were founded with the aim of improving this situation. The National Association for the Advancement of Colored People (NAACP – founded in 1909) was a pressure group which concentrated on using the courts to make white authorities do what the law said they were supposed to do. Marcus Garvey's Universal Negro Improvement Association (UNIA – founded in 1914) was more interested in getting African Americans to ignore white society and do things for themselves.

Another breakthrough was finally made in the 1960s, when successful new campaigns were mounted by groups like Martin Luther King's Southern Christian Leadership

American civil rights campaigners during the famous March 1965 protest march from Selma to Montgomery.

21

Conference to ensure that African American civil and voting rights were as real in practice as they were in theory. But even this was not the end of the story. At the end of the 20th century, African Americans were still more likely to be poor and unemployed than white Americans, and further campaigns in the cause of true racial equality seemed inevitable.

Slavery today

During World War II, foreigners were used as slave labour in German industry, and after the war the **United Nations** redefined a slave as anyone who was forced to work for a particular employer until such time as the employer said he or she could leave. By the end of the 20th century, it was estimated that around 200 million people in the developing world were in this position. Most of them had been forced to borrow money in order to feed themselves, and now had no choice but to work for the lender.

The Anti-Slavery Society, which still exists, has intervened successfully on behalf of such people. In the 1970s, for example, it helped to free an Amazonian tribe, the Andoke, from debt slavery to rubber merchants.

⑤ Women and children last

In 1833 – the year **slavery** was finally abolished in the British Empire – British women were legally little better off than slaves. Children of four worked down mines, and old people who were unable to work or afford medical care faced spending the final years of their lives in poverty and pain. This state of affairs was gradually addressed over the next century and a half. Just as one series of campaigns had forced the USA to reduce racial inequality, so other series of campaigns, in western countries such as the USA, the UK and Australia, persuaded governments to reduce gender and age inequality.

Women

In 19th-century Britain, women were not allowed to hold official jobs or enter any **profession** except teaching or nursing. They could work in one of the many factories which had been thrown up by the **Industrial Revolution**, but the working conditions were frequently appalling, in spite of the various Factory Acts introduced by the government to improve them. Even in the home, women had no right to any property which they brought into a marriage, and no right to keep or even see their children in the event of their marriage breaking down.

How were women to improve this state of affairs? Only by forcing the government to introduce new laws, and for this they needed suffrage, or the right to vote. As early as 1792, the English feminist Mary Wollstonecraft had argued for women's suffrage, but it was not until late in the 19th century that campaigns began in several countries with this aim in mind. In the UK, the fight was eventually led by a campaigning group called the Women's Social and Political Union (WSPU). This was founded in 1903 at the Manchester home of Emmeline Pankhurst, and was led by her and her eldest daughter Christabel.

Over the next twelve years the British **suffragettes** fought a many-sided campaign. They talked to those they knew who might have influence, and they brought constant pressure to bear on the all-male government and **Parliament** by making speeches and holding demonstrations.

They challenged government ministers in the street and turned up on their front doorsteps. They advertised their cause through badges and posters, stencilled slogans and pavement paintings. When they were arrested they went on **hunger strike**. In every peaceful way they could think of, the suffragettes placed their case before the public and the government.

When this failed to produce the desired result, they adopted a more violent strategy, although they only aimed their violence against property. Empty houses and post boxes were set on fire, railway seats slashed, telephone wires cut. One woman threw herself in front of the King's horse during the 1913 Derby, and was trampled to death. When World War I interrupted their campaign, the suffragette leaders went out of their way to prove that women could take over the jobs of men who were now in uniform. In 1918 their campaign finally paid off, and women over 30 were given the vote. Ten years later the age limit was reduced to 21, and women finally had voting equality with men.

Suffragette Emily Wilding Davison is killed after throwing herself in front of the King's horse at the Derby in 1913.

Winning the vote for women, like the freeing of the slaves in the USA, was both an end and a beginning. It closed one chapter of the struggle for gender equality, but made possible the opening of others – on, for example, equal pay, equal educational opportunities, contraception and **childcare provision**. The women's suffrage campaign, like the later **feminist** campaigns of the 1970s and 1980s, was part of an ongoing campaign for **gender equality**.

Children

The Factory Acts and the Mines Act which Lord Shaftesbury and like-minded friends persuaded the government to introduce in the 1830s and 1840s, set limits on the age at which children could be employed in various jobs. Children under nine, for example, could now no longer be employed in factories. This was progress of a sort, but it was 1901 before the age limit was raised to twelve. Throughout the 19th century, children continued to live and work in atrocious conditions.

It was not only their employers that the children had to fear – as late as 1884 the authorities had no power to prevent ill-treatment by parents. It was in that year that the National Society for the Prevention of Cruelty to Children (NSPCC) was formed.

Helping the old

Old age pensions are now an accepted part of life in many countries, but they rarely cover more than the bare necessities of life. There is still much poverty among large sections of the elderly population. In the UK there are several groups which campaign on behalf of the old and offer practical help to those in most need. The two best known are Age Concern, which took that name in 1971, but which was originally formed to help the old during the war, and Help the Aged, which was set up in 1961 to tackle the problems of poverty and isolation among the elderly.

The first five years of NSPCC campaigning persuaded the government to pass a Prevention of Cruelty to Children Act. Fifteen years after that, NSPCC officers were given the power to take children into care if a magistrate agreed.

A cartoon drawn by the Englishman George Cruikshank in 1869, showing the cruel way children were treated at the time. The NSPCC was founded a few years later to campaign for children's rights.

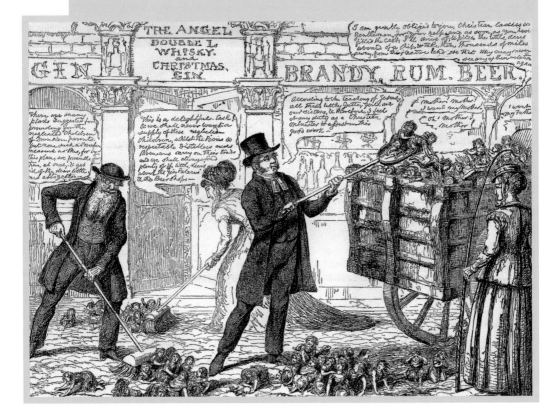

World War I produced suffering for many, but one woman, Eglantyne Jebb, was deeply moved by the sight of starving children in Austria after the war. She launched an appeal for help called the Save the Children Fund, and soon an organization of that name was collecting and delivering relief supplies all across Europe.

In 1923 Jebb wrote a Children's Charter, listing the rights she thought every child should have, and her words were later included as part of the **United Nations** Charter. In 1989 the UN went even further, adopting a Convention on the Rights of the Child.

Children learn how to brush their teeth with green twigs at a school run by the Save the Children Fund in Nepal.

By the end of the 20th century, the original Save the Children Fund had projects up and running in 50 of the world's poorer countries. By this time it was only one of several groups campaigning around the world for the rights of children.

Children in need

Each year in the UK, BBC TV devotes a whole evening to the Children in Need campaign. Various celebrities ask the watching audience for donations, and films are shown to illustrate how the money raised in the previous year has been spent.

6 Helping the less fortunate

Over the last two centuries the economies of Europe (particularly north-western Europe), North America and Australasia have grown at a tremendous speed, and the general level of prosperity has increased in leaps and bounds. However, there have been many people who have been unable to share in this rising prosperity, and who, for one reason or another, have been unable to speak for themselves. As a result, a wide variety of campaigning groups have been formed to speak for them.

In the 19th century

In the early 19th century, much attention was paid to the conditions in which people worked, and people like Lord Shaftesbury successfully campaigned for new laws – such as the Factory and Mines Acts – which gradually improved those conditions. In the second half of the century, the new workers' organizations – the **trade unions** (labour unions in the USA) – took over the job of campaigning for better pay and conditions, a job which they still perform today.

Of course, those in jobs were unlikely to be the poorest members of society. Those without jobs were allowed to work for their food in what were called **workhouses**, but these were not much better than prisons. No real attempt was made to tackle poverty as such, because the authorities were afraid that if they made such places too comfortable, the workers would stop working. Some individuals campaigned for changes, but with little success. Many people shared the authorities' belief that the poor had only themselves to blame for their poverty.

Those campaigns which were successful tended to concentrate on particular problems which the poor faced. One such problem was being trapped in a life of crime, and it was here that Elizabeth Fry made her mark, campaigning for the right of prisoners to educate themselves in prison.

Two famous men were provoked into action by the widespread problem of homelessness. In the early 1860s George Peabody, a successful American businessman who lived in England, funded the building of large numbers of spacious houses and apartments – the Peabody Dwellings – which ordinary working people could afford. Later in the same decade, a young doctor named Thomas Barnardo, horrified by the number of homeless children he discovered in London, opened the first of over a hundred homes for them.

Houses built by the Peabody Association in the mid-19th century on Blackfriars Road, London. George Peabody wanted to provide affordable housing for ordinary working people.

The **mentally ill** and **mentally handicapped** were other groups unable to speak for themselves. Philippe Pinel was a French doctor in the late 18th century who managed to persuade the authorities that mental patients in asylums should be treated with kindness, and should not, as was then usually the case, be kept in chains.

Two Americans, Benjamin Rush and Dorothea Dix, were among those who spread word of Pinel's success in France through their own country and the rest of Europe. By the end of the 19th century, most mental patients were still locked up, but their conditions had been much improved.

In the 20th century

In the 20th century the harsher forms of poverty – the lack of basic human needs like food, clothing and shelter – became rarer (though by no means unknown) in the richer countries of the world. The trade unions managed to keep up the wages of those in work, and a whole range of **benefits**, such as unemployment benefit, sickness benefit and **old age pensions**, were introduced to protect those who, through no fault of their own, were unable to earn a decent living for themselves or save for their retirement.

However, many of the specific problems associated with poverty remained. Both old and new pressure groups campaigned to solve or reduce them. As the 21st century began, both the Peabody Dwellings and Barnardo's homes were still providing much-needed services. At the same time, newer organizations, such as the pressure groups Shelter and Crisis, were campaigning on behalf of the homeless population.

An early
Dr Barnardo's
children's home in
London. Barnado
was a doctor who
wanted to help
homeless children.

The same pattern was repeated in mental health care. In 1946 two campaigning groups were founded in Britain. After several letters from worried mothers of mentally handicapped children appeared in the magazine *Nursery World*, a series of meetings were held, which resulted in the founding of the Royal Society for Mentally Handicapped Children and Adults (MENCAP). In the same year, other people came together to form the National Association for Mental Health (MIND). Over the last half-century, both organizations have campaigned effectively for better services and better understanding of those they represent, raising funds through street collections and events, and making full use of the modern media to spread their message.

The power of TV

The participants of the 2001 Big Brother series in Australia took part in a '40 Hour Famine' for the charity World Vision. This helped inspire more than 340,000 young Australians to give up food for 40 hours to raise funds for people in Asia and Africa who are suffering from hunger.

The treatment of animals

Many campaigns in the 19th and 20th centuries were fought to improve the way that people treat other people. During that same period, there was also a growing recognition that human beings are not the only species worthy of consideration. There has, particularly over the last 30 years, been a rapid increase in the number of campaigns to improve the way that people treat animals.

Animal cruelty and animal rights

In the early 19th century, campaigners worked to prevent, or at least reduce, cruelty to animals. The Royal Society for the Prevention of Cruelty to Animals (RSPCA), which was founded in 1824, campaigned to convince people that it was wrong to mistreat animals, and prosecuted those who continued to do so. It persuaded governments to ban bear-baiting and cock-fighting, fought long and hard to reduce the ill-treatment of horses, and was largely responsible for the comprehensive Protection of Animals Act of 1911. Its successes were widely admired, and similar organizations were set up in many other countries.

Groups like the RSPCA objected to the cruel treatment of animals, but they did not claim that animals had equal rights to humans. They did not, for example, criticize the eating of meat. They merely insisted that the animals in question should be raised and killed without unnecessary cruelty.

Setting an example

'The greatness of a nation and its moral progress can be judged by the way its animals are treated.'

(Indian leader Mohandas Gandhi, who spent much of his life trying to improve the way humans treated each other)

In 1892 an Englishman named Henry Salt wrote *Animal Rights in Relation to Social Progress*, the first book on animal rights. He claimed that humans should treat animals with mutual respect. He thought that no human being is justified as regarding any animal whatsoever as a meaningless automaton (robot), to be worked, or tortured, or eaten, as the case may be, for the mere object of satisfying the wants or whims of mankind.

This was a far stronger message than the one delivered by the anti-cruelty campaigners. If Salt and his later followers had their way, human beings would have to make big changes in the way they lived. This would include how they grew their food, what they ate and wore, how scientific research was conducted, even the way many of them entertained themselves.

Recent campaigns

More than a century after Salt published his book, his belief that animals should have equal rights to humans is still shared by only a small minority. Most people around the world continue to eat meat and fish when they can afford it. But the minority which came to share Salt's views has been influential – in the early 21st century animals, though far from equal, are definitely more equal than they were, and many types of treatment which were once considered acceptable no longer seem so.

A fur coat was a highly desirable item to own until the 1970s, but a campaign which highlighted the cruelties involved in catching and breeding the animals involved, and the threat posed to rare species, soon changed that. A famous advertisement showed a fashion model wearing a fur coat with the phrase 'It takes up to 40 dumb animals to make a fur coat. But only one to wear it.' The number of fur coats in the shops dropped dramatically.

Animals have been used in scientific testing for centuries, usually to find out whether new products might harm human beings. Many scientists claim that this testing – or vivisection, as it often called – is necessary for the

It takes up to 40 dumb animals to make a fur coat.

But only one to wear it.

LYNX

ou don't want millions of anim...ort...killed in leg-hold...os,don't buy a fur c...

protection of human health, but others disagree. Some claim that many tests are unnecessary, while those who believe in equal animal rights argue that humans have no right to safeguard their health at the expense of animal health. Groups as different as the Anti-Vivisection Society, the Body Shop cosmetics chain and the Animal Liberation Front have been involved in campaigns to either reduce or completely stop the use of animals in experiments.

There have been many other campaigns against cruelty to animals: against the way farm animals are treated, against the use of animals for entertainment in zoos and circuses, against sports like fox-hunting, rodeos, bull-fighting, shooting and fishing which involve the ill-treatment or murder of animals. There have also been campaigns to save whole species, like the tiger and white rhinoceros, from the final cruelty – extinction.

Different tactics

Many organizations working in the field of animal rights campaign in the usual way, writing letters and making appeals on TV, issuing pamphlets, books and videos, seeking to persuade both the general public and those in influential positions that a particular change in the law would be a good thing. However, animal rights is a subject which creates a lot of passion, and other organizations prefer a more direct approach. This can be peaceful and more or less legal, like the attempts by **hunt saboteurs** to interrupt fox hunts, or violent and completely illegal, like sending letter bombs to scientists involved in animal experimentation.

A line of rabbits, their bodies enclosed in metal cases, are used to test drugs for possible ill-effects. Many groups are campaigning to stop experiments like this.

⑧ Conflicting interests

All governments occasionally bring in a new law which favours one section of society over another. If the section which dislikes the law is large and powerful enough to think it has a chance of reversing the process, it may well start a campaign to do so. If opinion is divided along fairly equal lines, and both sides to the argument have a great deal of support, then both may produce campaigns, one for changing the law and one for keeping it as it is.

The Anti-Corn Law League

The campaign against the British Corn Laws of the early 19th century was a classic example of conflicting interests at work. The various Corn Laws – some were introduced as early as the 12th century – made foreign corn more expensive by charging a **tariff** on each shipment which was imported. This in turn allowed British landowners and farmers to keep their prices high. The Corn Laws worked in their favour, and in the early 19th century they were still the dominant force in **Parliament**.

However, as the British population expanded and the country industrialized, those same laws worked against the interests of a growing majority of the population. The Corn Laws kept bread prices higher than necessary even in years of good harvests at home. In years of bad harvests, they led to shortages, rocketing prices, and real hardship.

The Anti-Corn Law League was founded in Manchester in 1839. It was supported by the middle and working classes who lived in the cities, and who were fed up with paying too much for their bread. Meetings were held throughout the country, pamphlets distributed, politicians asked for their support. It was a classic single-issue campaign, with one aim and one aim only. In 1845 the pressure finally paid off. Following another bad harvest in England, and with famine looming in Ireland, Prime Minister Sir Robert Peel decided that the country could no longer afford its tax on foreign corn. The Corn Laws were abandoned.

A meeting of the Anti-Corn Law League in London's Covent Garden, May 1845. The League was a single-issue campaign group which fought to lower the price of bread.

Gun control

In the case of the Corn Laws, the needs of a growing majority eventually took preference over the needs of a diminishing minority, but sometimes conflicting interests remain locked in more or less equal combat. The issue of gun control in the present-day USA provides a good example of this.

The National Rifle Association (NRA) was founded in 1871 to defend the right of Americans – as written in the constitution – to own guns. By the end of the 20th century it employed over 350 people and had a membership of around three million. The NRA has a whole department devoted to lobbying politicians, and each year it sends out more than a million pamphlets arguing its case. In 1976 it set up a separate organization, the Political Victory Fund, which gives money to political candidates who support its aims.

There are a number of groups campaigning for tighter gun controls, but Handgun Control, Inc. (HCI) and the Coalition to Stop Handgun Violence (CSGV) are probably the most important. Both were set up in 1974, and both have seen their memberships rise with the number of incidents featuring gun-related violence. However, HCI and CSGV lack the financial power of the NRA, and they have a harder job getting their message across. No significant laws have been introduced across the USA, but tighter gun controls have been introduced in several states.

American actor and gun-supporter Charlton Heston addresses a meeting of the NRA in May 1999. This group campaigns to defend the right of Americans to own guns.

Sacrificing the few for the many

Most people believe that a new law or project which sacrifices the interests of the many in the interests of a few is unacceptable, and campaigns which seek to oppose that law or project are often successful. More common perhaps are those new laws and projects which sacrifice the interests of the few to the interests of the many, and campaigns which seek to oppose them have a much harder job on their hands.

If, for example, local or central government decides that a new town must be built in the countryside, those few people who already live in that area will be told that the good of the nation must come before their desire to keep their community the way it is. In the same way, people in a particular part of a large city may be told that the city needs a new road, and that their houses and community must be sacrificed in order to improve the country's transport system. In both situations, people will probably form pressure groups to campaign against the changes. Their chances of stopping the project are rarely high, but such campaigns can at least ensure that people whose lives are disrupted receive adequate compensation.

Not in my back yard!

Some campaigns to prevent unwanted waste dumps, incinerators or nuclear power stations have been called 'not in my back yard' (NIMBY) campaigns, because the campaigners are only opposed to such projects when they are personally affected by them. For example, responsible campaigners against the building of an incinerator will offer different suggestions for getting rid of the rubbish, not simply hope that the incinerator will be built in someone else's back yard.

Protesters in a British campaign take to the trees to prevent them from being cut down to build a new road.

Matters of life and death

Some of the most passionate and long-lasting campaigns have been fought over issues which involve the taking of human life. The idea that human life is sacred has a long history – most of the major religious books contain at least one passage prohibiting killing. In spite of this, almost all societies have considered execution a suitable punishment for some crimes and war an acceptable means of settling disputes. In recent times many people have argued that abortion, or putting an end to unwanted pregnancies, should also be seen as the taking of human life.

Capital punishment

In the mid-18th century, killing convicted offenders, or **capital punishment**, took place in every country in the world, often for the most trivial offences. In Britain, for example, people were executed for stealing just a few pence or damaging London's Westminster Bridge.

A public execution outside Newgate Prison in London. December 1809. Capital punishment was abolished in the UK in 1965, after a lengthy campaign.

In 1764 an Italian named Cesare Beccaria wrote and published a pamphlet, *On Crimes and Punishment*, which convinced a number of people in many countries that legal executions were wrong. Emperor Joseph of Austria was so taken by Beccaria's arguments that in 1781 he gave the order that his own country should be the first to abolish capital punishment. Six years later, on the other side of the Atlantic Ocean, the Philadelphia Society for Alleviating the Miseries of Public Prisons became the first group in the USA to campaign against the death penalty.

Through the 19th century, various individuals and groups promoted the same cause. Some met with success – Holland and Venezuela had abolished capital punishment by 1870 – but most were frustrated by failure. Many countries only kept the death penalty for the most serious crimes – usually, murder and **treason** – but they did keep it. Some even continued with public executions. In France, the last of these took place as recently as 1939.

In the UK, capital punishment was finally abolished in 1965, after a campaign led by the Labour MP Sydney Silverman and the publisher Victor Gollancz. Their cause was helped by the shift in public opinion which followed the discovery in 1953 that an innocent man, Timothy Evans, had been hanged three years earlier. France gave up legal executions in 1981, but in America some states continue to use the death penalty and others have brought it back after periods in which it had not been used.

Abortion

In recent decades abortion, or the deliberate ending of pregnancy, has become a major campaigning issue. Some people believe that abortions should be available to women who want them, and they argue that women have the right to decide what goes on in their own bodies, including whether or not to see a pregnancy through to birth.

41

Such beliefs fuelled the campaigns in the 1960s and 1970s which paved the way for the legalization of abortion in countries like the UK (1967) and the USA (1973).

Other people argue that women do not have the right to choose whether or not to give birth. They say that abortion is the murder of an unborn child. This is the position taken by the Roman Catholic church, and one which has been supported around the world in so-called 'right to life' campaigns.

Today, some countries allow abortion for any woman who wants it, some only allow it in particular cases (after rape, or when, for health reasons, the mother's life is threatened by the pregnancy), and some disallow it completely. Abortion remains a highly controversial issue, both in countries where it is legal and in countries where it is not.

Pacifism

Opposition to war is probably as old as humankind, but the first truly pacifist movement was Buddhism, and King Asoka, who ruled part of India in the 3rd century BC, was probably the first ruler to renounce war as a means of settling disputes. Few followed his example, however. There were always individuals prepared to speak out against war, and even large movements – often associated with one or other of the world's religions – who campaigned against it. However, for most of the next 2000 years, states, rulers and peoples fought and killed each other with great regularity.

In the 19th and early 20th centuries, pacifists tried to promote peace by campaigning for those things which they believed made wars less likely. These included fewer weapons, more **democracy**, and international courts to which states could take their grievances. When wars did break out, pacifists refused to fight, and many went to prison for their refusal. Some, like the Indian leader Gandhi, were prepared to share the dangers by serving as front-line medical staff, but were not prepared to carry a weapon or kill their fellow human beings.

Since World War II, pacifism has been mostly associated with opposition to weapons capable of mass murder (particularly nuclear weapons) and opposition to particular wars. The **Campaign for Nuclear Disarmament** (**CND**) was founded in the UK in 1958, and that year held its first march from London to the Atomic Weapons Research Establishment at Aldermaston, some 50 miles to the west. Since then CND, like other anti-nuclear weaponry movements around the world, has continued to campaign, as yet unsuccessfully, for the complete abolition of nuclear weapons.

The women of Greenham Common

In 1980 it was announced that US **cruise missiles** were to be sited at the Greenham Common Royal Air Force base in south-east England. In the following September, a peace march was held from Cardiff to Greenham Common, and a large number of women set up a peace camp outside the base. This camp, and even some of its original inhabitants, remained in place until the missiles were finally removed in 1991. There were regular rallies and well-publicized break-ins, all of which kept both the camp and the issue of cruise missiles in the news.

The women of Greenham Common.

US involvement in the Vietnam War in the 1960s and early 1970s saw the growth of a large peace movement in the USA itself. This movement, though it failed to stop the war, undoubtedly made it harder for the government and military to conduct the war as they wished. Similar campaigns may have helped to restrain the American and British conduct of wars in the Gulf (1991) and Afghanistan (2001).

Anti–Vietnam War protesters in Washington DC on 24 May 1970. Three weeks earlier, four fellow campaigners had been shot dead by National Guardsmen at Kent State University, Ohio.

10 Single-issue political parties

Generally speaking, political parties are not founded to campaign on a single issue. On the contrary, they are usually based on a particular way of looking at the world, and how that way of looking can be applied across the whole range of social, political and economic issues. A **socialist**, for example, will want to see socialist ideas applied to everything from health care to defence.

The only notable exceptions to this rule, at least until recently, have been the **nationalist** parties which have sprung up in all parts of the world. These have all concentrated on a single issue – some kind of self-government for their nation.

Nationalist parties

For much of the 20th century, several European states ruled **colonial territories** around the world, and inside these territories groups organized themselves into nationalist parties in order to campaign for independence. The members of such parties had their own ideas on the range of social and economic issues which would face their countries after independence, and so, in a sense, a real political party was already growing inside the single-issue nationalist party. Once independence was achieved, a party like the Indian Congress Party had to change from a single-issue nationalist party into an ordinary political party with policies covering the full range of relevant issues.

The European powers were also faced with nationalist demands closer to home. In regions like Scotland, Wales, Brittany and the Basque country, some of which had been conquered many centuries earlier, people demanded forms of self-government which ranged from their own **parliament** to complete independence. The Scottish National Party (SNP), for example, won its first seat in the UK's Parliament in 1945, and by the 1970s had increased its representation to eleven MPs.

The SNP continued to campaign for independence, but since it now represented Scottish voters in Parliament, it also developed policies on all the other issues which affected them.

The opening of a Scottish Parliament in 1999, and the devolution, or passing down, of powers to this Parliament over many areas of Scottish life, further emphasized the dual nature of parties like the SNP. On the one hand it behaved like a normal multi-issue party, and on the other it remained focused on the single overriding issue of independence.

In September 1997 Scottish nationalists gathered in Stirling to celebrate a 700-year-old victory over the English at Stirling Bridge. Soon after this, the Scottish people voted for the establishment of their own parliament in Edinburgh.

Environmentalist or green parties

In recent years, concern over the environment has led to the creation of several **green** political parties, which put forward candidates at elections like any other political party. Some consider these are single-issue parties, but their supporters argue that most, if not all, political decisions have environmental consequences, and that therefore green parties are multi-issue parties. Like conservatives or socialists, **environmentalists** have applied their way of looking at the world to a whole range of issues.

A conference of the German Green Party. At its peak in 1987, this party held 46 seats in the German parliament.

No green party has yet won a majority of votes, but some, like the German green party (Die Grünen), have shared power with other parties in national government. In most countries where they have had some electoral success, green parties have acted as pressure groups inside parliaments, giving their support to other, more popular parties who most closely share their aims.

No dams

In 1981, a campaign began to stop the damming of the Franklin River in Tasmania, Australia. Celebrities such as Professor David Bellamy became involved in the peaceful direct action known as the Franklin Blockade. In the federal election in 1983, the Tasmanian Wilderness Society ran a strong 'vote for the Franklin' campaign, and later analysis showed that this campaign had been crucial in the outcome of the election. After accepting victory, Bob Hawke, the new prime minister, announced that the dam would not proceed. The case was a landmark in Australian environmental and constitutional history. It established the Commonwealth government's power to protect the national environment on issues of international importance.

International campaigns

During the last quarter of the 20th century, advances in telecommunications and computing allowed huge **multinational corporations** to extend their operations around the world. This **globalization** was further speeded up in the 1990s by the collapse of **communism** in eastern Europe and the partial opening up of China to Western business.

Globalization brought many changes. People generally became more aware of what was happening in the rest of the world. Power shifted from national governments to the multi-national corporations, and environmental problems which were truly international in scope were created, or got worse. International causes were recognized and campaigns were needed – and became possible – because of these changes.

Saving the environment

The most noticeable of the international groups formed over the last 30 years have been those campaigning on behalf of the environment. There has been a growing awareness of the threats to the very basis of life on Earth posed by human economic activity. These include the thinning of the ozone layer through the use of chemicals called chlorofluorocarbons, the **global warming** effect produced by other gas **emissions**, and the reduction of **biodiversity** caused by too much hunting, fishing and tree-felling. These threats were behind the birth of groups like the World Wide Fund for Nature (set up in 1961 as the World Wildlife Fund), Friends of the Earth (1971) and Greenpeace (1971), which now have members all over the world.

The issues these groups deal with are international problems, and in some ways can only be solved by international action, by governments coming together and sharing necessary sacrifices. Groups like Greenpeace have kept environmental problems in the public eye, and this in turn has kept up the pressure on governments and businesses. They have done this in a variety of ways: by holding meetings and advertising, by sponsoring research and supplying knowledgeable speakers whenever schools or the media wanted them, or by taking direct action when it seemed appropriate. Greenpeace activists, for example, have often tried to put their bodies in the way of action which they consider harmful to the environment, like nuclear testing or the killing of whales.

Environmental organizations have also made a point of encouraging individual members of the public to live environmentally responsible lives. Using cars only when necessary and not using sprays which contain chlorofluorocarbons are only two ways we can all help.

Rights for the developing world

Many international campaigns are about extending rights which have already been won in the developed world to the rest of humankind. Ill-treatment of people on grounds of gender, age or race has not disappeared in the richer countries, but it has grown less serious than it once was, and much less serious than it still is in most of the poorer countries. The same can be said of poverty and the lack of political rights. Both are still found in the richer countries, but are a far greater problem for the inhabitants of the poorer countries.

Victims of famine in Ethiopia await the distribution of food provided by an international relief agency.

The same conditions which inspired many 19th-century reformers to campaign for change in Europe and North America can now be found in the developing world in the early 21st century.

Some campaigning groups – **relief organizations** like Oxfam, War on Want and Christian Aid – offer continuing help to the whole developing world, while others are more selective. Bob Geldof's 1984 Band Aid campaign was organized to help the victims of a famine in Ethiopia, and the annual Comic Relief campaigns, which grew out of Band Aid, are aimed at improving the situation of the poorest people in the developing world. Amnesty International was founded in 1961 to campaign for the release of prisoners of conscience – people imprisoned for expressing their political beliefs – around the world. Local groups organized letter-writing campaigns on behalf of particular prisoners, which made it harder for governments to ill-treat them, and in many cases such prisoners were released to spare the governments' embarrassment. Forty years later, Amnesty is still campaigning, and still issuing its influential annual report on how the world's governments are treating their political opponents.

At a concert organized by Amnesty International, Chilean mothers hold up photographs of children who 'disappeared' under the regime of General Pinochet.

Other campaigning groups have argued that all these problems really add up to just one – the denial of **human rights**. If everyone was promised the same rights as everyone else, then discrimination on grounds of gender, age or race would disappear, and so would political abuses and economic exploitation. Over the years, many individuals and groups in many countries have campaigned for human rights, and this pressure persuaded the **United Nations** to prepare a Universal Declaration of Human Rights. Released in 1948, this included a comprehensive list of political, social and economic rights, many of which are still not enjoyed by large numbers of the world's population. Many countries now have groups which campaign for the spread of human rights.

Excerpts from the Universal Declaration of Human Rights

'Article 5: No one shall be subjected to torture or to cruel, inhuman or degrading treatment or punishment.

'Article 25 (1): Everyone has the right to a standard of living adequate for the health and well-being of himself and of his family, including food, clothing, housing and medical care and necessary social services, and the right to security in the event of unemployment, sickness, disability, widowhood, old age or other lack of livelihood in circumstances beyond his control.'

Consumer power

In the past, pressure groups in democracies tried to convince the public of the rightness of their causes, knowing full well that politicians were likely to adopt their cause if it looked likely to win them votes. With globalization, however, politicians and national governments have lost power to the multinational corporations. They often cannot deliver what the pressure groups and public want them to deliver. In such cases, public pressure has to be applied to the corporations themselves.

There have been several recent examples of such campaigns. Trainer manufacturers have been forced by the exposure of abuses to improve working conditions in their factories in the developing world, and well-publicized **boycotts** of filling stations have persuaded oil companies to take a more environment-friendly approach. In the end, individuals can protest against the actions or behaviour of a particular company by simply refusing to buy its products. The campaigner's job is simply to make sure that the individual has the information he or she needs to take such decisions.

Greenpeace campaigners in Switzerland, protesting at what they see as Shell's involvement in the murder of human rights activists in Nigeria. They are urging consumers to boycott the company.

12 So, what are campaigns and causes?

Campaigns come in all shapes and sizes. Some are inspired, led and run by a single person, while others involve people of all nationalities working together in groups aimed at the same target. Some enjoy complete success, while some are utterly defeated. Some simply keep going, making occasional small advances, while others, frustrated by failure or government unwillingness to listen, spill over into law-breaking and violence.

Causes, too, come in bewildering variety. Some, like the blocking of a new road or the ending of fox-hunting, can be fought to a satisfactory conclusion. The transport ministry which wants the road can decide that public opposition is too strong, and cancel the project; a government can pass a law making fox-hunting illegal and take steps to enforce it. Those campaigning for such causes can then congratulate themselves and disband their groups.

Other campaigns, like the ending of cruelty to children or animals, are much harder to bring to a successful conclusion. People cannot agree what cruelty is. Different cultures have different standards. Laws can be passed, but private behaviour is always difficult to police. In such cases, campaigners keep watch and keep calling for higher standards. If, ten or twenty years down the line, fewer children or animals are abused, then that is success of a sort.

What most causes and campaigns share is a feeling that something is wrong. Men and women have reached that point where they say 'enough', where they feel that they have no choice but to try and persuade their fellow human beings to do things differently.

Artists and organizers gather on stage at the end of the 1985 Live Aid concert, which raised enormous amounts of money for the developing world.

Taking part

A positive feature of such campaigns is they allow individuals to take part in the political process, and to make their voices heard on subjects which they feel strongly about. This is important for democracy, which otherwise can mean little more than casting a vote every few years for the political party which seems the most sympathetic to one's own ideas. Individuals can join political parties, attend local meetings and take part in discussions, but often there is actually little to do, and little sense that one is making a difference.

Campaigning groups, by contrast, offer individuals the chance to get directly involved in what they feel passionate about. They can write letters, research and write pamphlets, hold demonstrations, collect donations in the street. They can take direct action, refusing to buy the products of a particular company or lying in front of bulldozers which are trying to clear the way for a new road.

Party politics are often complicated, involving all sorts of compromises with one's principles, but campaign goals are usually clear and simple. If the goal is to monitor, reduce and eventually eliminate some form of abuse to humans, animals or the environment, then the individual has the satisfaction of acting according to his or her principles, and doing a job which needs doing. If the goal is actually reachable in the short term – like stopping the building of a road – then success will bring a real sense of achievement. Either way, the individual will know that his or her voice has been heard, that he or she has made a difference.

Cheers!

Not all campaigns are political. The Campaign for Real Ale (CAMRA) was founded in 1971 by four friends holidaying together in Ireland. They were upset that traditional beers – those which continue to ferment in a cask – were being driven out of existence by mass-produced pasteurized beers, and decided to do something about it. Within ten years their organization had over 30,000 members, and they were able to publish an annual *Good Beer Guide* and sponsor an annual Great British Beer Festival.

Timeline

1764	Cesare Beccaria condemns the death penalty in *On Crimes and Punishment*
1772	British court frees a runaway slave
1780	Pennsylvania becomes the first US state to begin freeing slaves
1781	Austria abolishes **capital punishment**
1787	Society for Abolition of the Slave Trade founded in London
1789	French Revolution begins
1790s	Tuke and Pinel pioneer new treatment for the **mentally ill**
1792	Mary Wollstonecraft argues for **gender equality** in *Vindication of the Rights of Woman*
1807	**Slave trade** abolished in all British possessions
1810s	Elizabeth Fry campaigns for prison reform
1823	Anti-**Slavery** Society founded in UK
1824	Society for the Prevention of Cruelty to Animals founded. It became the Royal Society – RSPCA – in 1838.
1832	Anti-Slavery Society founded in USA
1833	First Factory Act to regulate working conditions is introduced in UK
	Abolition of slavery in the British Empire
1834	Dorothea Dix campaigns in USA on behalf of the poor, the mentally ill and prisoners
1838	Charles Dickens's *Nicholas Nickleby* is published
	Frederick Douglass escapes slavery, and begins a life-long campaign against it
1838–48	The Chartist campaign
1839–45	The Anti-Corn Law campaign
1859	John Brown is caught and hanged after seizing the armoury at Harpers Ferry, Virginia, USA
1860s	George Peabody builds low-cost housing in London
1861–65	American Civil War
1863	American slaves are freed
1867	Dr Barnardo builds first home for children in London's East End

1871	National Rifle Association (NRA) founded in USA
1884	National Society for Prevention of Cruelty to Children (NSPCC) founded in UK
1889	Protection of Children Act passed by British **Parliament**
1892	Henry Salt's *Animal Rights in Relation to Social Progress* is published
1903–14	Crucial years of the British **suffragette** campaign
1909	National Association for the Advancement of Colored People (NAACP) founded in USA
1911	Protection of Animals Act passed by British Parliament
1914	Universal Negro Improvement Association (UNIA) founded in USA
1914–18	World War I
1917	First **communist** revolution takes place in Russia
1918	British women over 30 are given the vote
1920–33	**Prohibition** of alcohol in the USA
1923	Eglantyne Jebb writes Children's Charter
1928	British women over 21 are given the vote
1929–33	The Great Depression
1934	Scottish National Party founded
1939–45	World War II
1942	Oxfam (Oxford Committee for Famine Relief) founded
1945	Christian Aid founded
1946	Royal Society for Mentally Handicapped Children and Adults (MENCAP) and the National Association for Mental Health (MIND) are founded
1947	Cold War begins
	UK gives independence to India (beginning of European decolonization)
1948	UN adopts Universal Declaration of Human Rights

1955–65	Crucial years of Civil Rights Movement in USA
1958	Campaign for Nuclear Disarmament (CND) founded
	First Aldermaston march
1961	Amnesty International founded
1965	Capital punishment abolished in Britain
1965–70	Anti-Vietnam War movement in US
1966	Shelter founded
1970	Band of Mercy (later, the Animal Liberation Front) founded
1971	Campaign for Real Ale (CAMRA) founded
1972	Coalition to Stop Handgun Violence (CSGV) and Handgun Control, Inc. (HCI) set up in USA
1973	US Supreme Court decision (Roe v. Wade) legalizes abortion in USA
1981	Capital punishment abolished in France
1984	Band Aid set up by Bob Geldof
1985	First year of Comic Relief
1987	The German green party Die Grünen wins 42 seats in German parliament
1989	The Convention of the Rights of the Child adopted by the UN
1989–91	The end of communism in Europe
1991	The Gulf War
1997	British government committed to ending fox-hunting is elected
1997	Kyoto Agreement to control the emissions which cause **global warming**

Further reading

Paul Brown *Greenpeace* (Exley, 1993)
Reg Grant *Amnesty International* (Franklin Watts, 2000)
Robin May *Pressure Groups* (Wayland, 1983)
Nina Morgan *Famous Campaigners for Change* (Wayland, 1993)
Michael Pollard *People Who Care* (Heinemann, 1991)
Paul Thomas *Campaigners* (Belitha, 1997)
Paul Wignall *Animal Rights* (Heinemann, 2000)

The End of Apartheid (Turning Points in History, Heinemann)
Chartism (History in Depth, Heinemann)
Britain and the Slave Trade (History in Depth, Heinemann)
The Environment and You (What's at Issue, Heinemann)
Prejudice and Difference (What's at Issue, Heinemann)
Animal Rights (What's at Issue, Heinemann)

Harriet Beecher Stowe *Uncle Tom's Cabin* (Wordsworth)
Charles Dickens *Nicholas Nickleby*
Charles Kingsley *The Water Babies* (Puffin Books)
Anna Sewell *Black Beauty* (Puffin Books)

Sources

Pressure Groups (HMSO, 1994)
Peter Joyce, *An Introduction to Politics* (Hodder & Stoughton, 1999)
David Selby, *Human Rights* (Cambridge University Press, 1987)

Websites

Amnesty International: www.amnesty.org.uk
Anti-Slavery Society: www.antislavery.org
Anti-Vivisection Society: www.cygnet.co.uk/navs
Age Concern: www.ageconcern.org.uk
Barnardos: www.barnardos.org.uk
Body Shop: www.the-body-shop.com

Campaign for Nuclear Disarmament: www.cnduk.org
Campaign for Real Ale: www.camra.org.uk
Children in Need: www.bbc.co.uk/cin
Christian Aid: www.christian–aid.org.uk
Comic Relief: www.comicrelief.org
Crisis: www.crisis.org.uk
Friends of the Earth: www.foe.co.uk
Greenpeace: www.greenpeace.org
Help The Aged: www.helptheaged.org.uk
Mencap: www.mencap.org.uk
MIND: www.mind.org.uk
National Society for the Prevention of Cruelty to Children:
    www.nspcc.org.uk
Oxfam: www.oxfam.org.uk
Peabody Trust: www.peabody.org.uk
Royal Society for the Prevention of Cruelty to Animals:
    www.rspca.co.uk
Royal Society for the Protection of Birds: www.rspb.org.uk
Save The Children: www.savethechildren.org.uk
Shelter: www.shelter.org.uk
War on Want: www.waronwant.org
Worldwide Fund for Nature (World Wildlife Fund):
    www.wwf–uk.org

Glossary

benefits payment made by government to those who, for various reasons, are unable to work

biodiversity the whole range of plant and animal life

boycott refusal to have dealings with

Campaign for Nuclear Disarmament (CND) organization formed in 1958 to campaign for the abolition of nuclear weapons

capital punishment use of the death penalty to punish crime

childcare provision creation of facilities for looking after children while their parents are at work

civil rights legal rights of all people to the same equal opportunities and benefits

colonies (usually poor) countries ruled by other (usually richer) countries

communism extreme form of socialism, in which property is held communally (in common) rather than individually

cruise missile jet-engined guided missile developed by the USA in the 1970s

debt slave someone who has to keep working in a particular situation in order to pay off a debt. Wages are often kept so low that the person has no chance of ever paying it off.

democracy political system in which governments are regularly elected by the mass of the people. Country in which this system exists

developing world countries that are making rapid changes from simple social and economic systems to wider prosperity

electorate those people entitled to vote in a specified area

emission something which is forced out

environmentalist someone who cares about, and is seeking to preserve, the natural environment

evangelist enthusiastic follower and promoter of Christianity

feminist someone who believes in, and argues for, equal rights for women

gender equality equality between males and females

global warming the gradual warming of the Earth's atmosphere, which is mostly caused by rising levels of carbon dioxide (also called the Greenhouse Effect)

globalization term describing the fast-moving spread of
   business, culture and communications across national
   boundaries in the late 20th and early 21st centuries

green in politics, giving a high priority to environmental matters

human rights rights which should belong to any person

hunger strike refusing to eat as a form of protest

hunt saboteur someone who tries to interfere with a hunt, by,
   for example, laying false trails

Industrial Revolution the change from a primarily agricultural
   economy to one based on large-scale production in factories
   which began, in England, in the 18th century

legal test case court case brought to test the current state of the
   law. Such cases can sometimes make it obvious to many people
   that the law is out of date and should be changed.

lobbyist someone who tries to persuade politicians that they
   should support a particular cause or course of action.
   Professional lobbyists are paid to do this on a full-time basis

mentally handicapped having a permanently lowered or
   undeveloped mental capacity

mentally ill having a mental condition which means you behave
   differently to other people

moral issue issue which raises fundamental questions about
   what is thought right and what is thought wrong

multinational corporation large business which operates in
   several countries

nationalism active promotion of national interest

old age pension regular payment made by the state to a person
   above a certain age

ozone layer layer of the Earth's atmosphere which absorbs most
   of the sun's harmful ultra-violet radiation

pacifism belief that war and violence can never be justified

parliament legislative assembly which has been at least partly
   elected

pasteurized partially sterilized by heating

petition a written request signed by many people

plaintiff individual (or group) who brings a case to court

plantation large farm growing a crop, like cotton, tobacco or sugar, which requires a large number of hand-pickers

profession traditionally, a job which requires a long period of academic or scientific training. Law, medicine and teaching are typical professions.

professional body organization set up to advance the interests of a profession

Prohibition the banning of alcohol in the USA between 1920 and 1933

Quaker member of the Christian group, the Society of Friends, which is particularly known for its devotion to peace

relief agency organization set up to relieve suffering (often in the developing world)

secret ballot system of voting in which no one knows which candidate or party any particular individual has voted for

slavery traditionally, the ownership of human beings by other human beings. It has recently been redefined by the United Nations to include those who are forced to continue working for a particular employer until such time as they have paid off their debt to that employer.

slave trade the buying and selling of slaves

socialism a set of political ideas which puts more stress on the needs of the community as a whole and less on the short-term wants or needs of the individual

suffragette campaigner for women's right to vote (women's suffrage)

trade unions organizations formed to protect and advance the pay and conditions of workers

treason taking action against one's own country

United Nations (UN) international organization set up in 1945 to promote peace and cooperation between states

vivisection experimentation with animals which involves dissection or other painful treatment

workhouses organizations which in the UK took in and fed poor people in return for work

Index

abortion 40, 41–2
Amnesty International 50
animal rights 10, 11, 17, 32–5, 53
Anti-Corn Law League 36, 37

Brown, John 13, 20

Campaign for Real Ale (CAMRA) 55
Campaign for Nuclear Disarmament (CND) 4, 5, 43
campaigning groups 13–14, 54
campaign funding 14
capital punishment 40–1
Chartism 9
child abuse 25–6, 53
child labour 23, 25
children's rights 27
civil rights 10, 14, 21
conflicting interests 36–9

democracy 8, 42, 54
demonstrations and marches 4, 15, 16, 23
developing world 49–51
Dickens, Charles 12

environmental issues 16, 17, 48–9
environmentalist parties 46–7

factory reforms 13, 23
fox-hunting 6, 8, 35, 53
Fry, Elizabeth 12, 17, 28
fur trade 33, 34

gender equality 23–5
globalization 11, 48, 51
government, influencing 7, 15, 19, 23, 37, 48
green politics 46–7
Greenham Common peace camp 43
Greenpeace 16, 17, 48–9, 52
gun control 37–8

homelessness 15, 28–9, 30, 31
human life 40–4
human rights 51

interest groups 7
international campaigns 11, 48–52

King Jr, Martin Luther 14, 16, 21

legal test cases 16
lobbyists 15, 37

mental illness 13, 29–30, 31
moral issues 11, 40–4
multi-issue campaigns 9
multinational corporations 48, 51–2

nationalist parties 45–6
non-governmental organizations (NGOs) 12
'not in my back yard' (NIMBY) campaigns 39

pacifism 42–4
physical action 16–17, 24, 35, 49, 54
political parties 7, 8, 11, 15, 45–7, 54
poverty 25, 28, 30, 49, 50
pressure groups 6, 7, 8, 15, 18, 19, 21, 30, 39, 51
prison reform 12, 28
prisoners of conscience 50
public awareness 12, 16–17, 19, 20, 51

racial equality 20–1
relief organizations 50
road building 10, 16, 39, 53, 54
RSPCA 32

Save the Children Fund 26, 27
Shelter 15, 31
single-issue campaigns 6, 7, 36
single-issue parties 45–7
slavery 10, 13, 18–20, 22
spokespeople 12, 17, 48–9
suffragettes 4, 7–8, 15, 23–4

temperance campaigns 7

violent action 17, 24, 35
vivisection 34
voting rights 4, 8, 9, 11, 21, 23–4

women's issues 4, 7–8, 11, 23–5
working pay and conditions 28, 30